DEBUTANTES AND THE LONDON SEASON

Lucinda Gosling

SHIRE PUBLICATIONS

Published in Great Britain in 2013 by Shire Publications Ltd, Midland House, West Way, Botley, Oxford OX2 0PH, United Kingdom.

43-01 21st Street, Suite 220B, Long Island City, NY 11101, USA.

E-mail: shire@shirebooks.co.uk   www.shirebooks.co.uk

A CIP catalogue record for this book is available from the British Library.

Shire Library no. 725   ISBN-13: 978 0 74781 219 7

Lucinda Gosling has asserted her right under the Copyright, Designs and Patents Act, 1988, to be identified as the author of this book.

Designed by Tony Truscott Designs, Sussex, UK and typeset in Perpetua and Gill Sans.

Printed in China through Worldprint Ltd.

13 14 15 16 17   10 9 8 7 6 5 4 3 2 1

COVER IMAGE
A Society ball held in a London mansion during the Season, 1928. Taken from *The Sphere* magazine, June 1928.

TITLE PAGE IMAGE
Court dress designs by Norman Hartnell, published in *Harper's Bazaar* in 1930. The mother's gown is of jewelled lace with a train of panne velvet, the debutante's is a 'souffle' of soft tulle frills, lightly jewelled with a train of transparent ruffled tulle – fabric which Hartnell approved of for young girls.

CONTENTS PAGE IMAGE
Stylish society at Ascot, incorporated into a vibrant masthead design by the artist 'Peter' for *The Bystander* in 1927.

ACKNOWLEDGEMENTS
I would like to thank Mary Evans Picture Library for their help with images for this book, Mike Daines for his permission to use his photograph of Queen Charlotte's Ball and my editor, Ruth Sheppard for her limitless patience and enthusiasm for the project.

PHOTOGRAPH ACKNOWLEDGEMENTS
Illustrated London News/Mary Evans Picture Library, front cover, pages 3, 4, 7, 8, 9, 11 (bottom), 12, 14 (bottom), 15, 16, 17, 19, 21, 26 (bottom), 30, 33 (top), 35, 36, 39, 41, 43, 44–5, 46, 50, 51, 54 top, 55, 57, 58, 60, 61, 62; Mary Evans Picture Library, pages 6 (bottom left), 18, 22, 40, 48, 52; Mike Daines, page 63; National Archives/Mary Evans Picture Library, page 14 (top); National Magazine Company/Mary Evans Picture Library, pages 1, 11, 20, 28, 29, 31, 38, 56; Ronald Grant/ Mary Evans Picture Library, page 59; Yevonde Portrait Archive/Mary Evans Picture Library, pages 32, 34. All other photographs are from the author's collection.

Shire Publications is supporting the Woodland Trust, the UK's leading woodland conservation charity, by funding the dedication of trees.

CONTENTS

The SPHERE

With which is
incorporated
Black & White
No.1430
June 18, 1927

SEASON
NUMBER
JUNE 1927

With all the
News
of the Week

Price
One Shilling

AN EXCLUSIVE CLUB

Each spring, from the mid-nineteenth century through to the beginning of the Second World War, as the blossom on the trees in London's exclusive squares unfurled, the well bred and well-heeled left their country estates and headed for the capital. Ahead of them travelled servants to prepare houses in readiness for their family's arrival. Across Mayfair, dustsheets were removed from heirloom furniture and windows were flung open to air fusty rooms. This flurry of activity prompted hotels, florists, hairdressers and caterers to place advertisements in society magazines, and to wait for their order books to fill up as invitations and RSVPs to endless balls, parties, evening receptions and events criss-crossed the city. This seasonal migration, these fevered preparations, heralded the start of what was known as the London Season; an intensive three-month social whirl participated in by those whose breeding, wealth and status marked them out as the so-called cream of British society.

'Society' once described the country's uppermost social ranks, a handful of ducal families sometimes described as the 'ton'. But an expanding population in the early nineteenth century led to an expansion of Society itself. Marital links were forged further down the chain, between the aristocracy and the landed gentry, and, in turn, the middle class, as younger sons of larger families cast their net wider in order to find a wife. In addition, increasing industrialisation created a growing contingent whose fortunes were made rather than inherited. These were 'new money' families; those who had the wealth but not, necessarily, the connections to gain admittance to Society.

H. V. Horton, writing a history of Mayfair in 1927, claimed that the origins of the Season lay in Mayfair's gentrification in the early eighteenth century, with the Season then lasting from December to the end of May. It did not follow the same rigid pattern as later centuries; Society followed the court and gravitated towards the great houses of political leaders but found entertainment at public spaces such as Vauxhall Pleasure Gardens or in Covent Garden theatres. A commentator in 1871 wrote of a previous

Opposite:
Front cover
of *The Sphere*'s
Season Number
from June 1927.
The quality weekly
magazines took an
unflagging interest
in The Season
and each year's
new crop of
debutantes.

Vauxhall Pleasure Gardens in the eighteenth century. Before the more intensive social segregation of the nineteenth century, the nobility would mix with lower classes at public entertainment venues.

generation 'that they [the very great] should partake of these pleasures in company that was always mixed and sometimes more than dubious as to its quality, supping, dancing, and playing at cards and hazard … and yet to the best of our knowledge no special harm or annoyance appears to have resulted from this singular comingling of the classes.' Advertising one's rank and station through segregation did not seem to occur to the eighteenth-century nobleman.

In the following century, socialising began increasingly to take on a more private form centred on parties in grand houses, meaning only those wealthy enough to own such residences, and only those who knew them, or knew someone who could introduce them, could take part. The grandest house of all, Buckingham Palace, operated the same system and only those who were introduced by someone who already had the 'entrée' could gain admittance. In many ways, the Season represented networking at the highest level, sub-consciously developed to filter out any undesirables and, in time, to bring together, under supervision, Society's unmarried daughters with potential husbands from the same elite stock.

The Season's timing shifted around before finally settling in spring and early summer. Roughly coinciding with the Parliamentary year, at first, when Parliament sat in February, gentlemen would bring their families with them to London, and in

Piccadilly, one of the smartest thoroughfares in London, pictured during the Season in 1895. The route was once lined with a number of aristocratic mansions.

time, it occupied the more concentrated period during the Parliamentary recess, which ran from spring to August. The timing provided a convenient period for this annual pilgrimage when a temporary easing of political obligation happily converged with social expediency. For the 120 years that followed Queen Victoria's accession, it became the way that Britain's upper classes spent May, June and July each year. In May 1886 an anonymous writer in *Harper's New Monthly Magazine* ran a feature on 'The London Season', introducing its readers to the giddy world of a high society summer. It began with the conundrum of finding a satisfactory definition for what was a vague and changeable phenomenon:

A house in prestigious Carlton House Terrace overlooking St James's Park at the height of the Season, showing guests arriving and others enjoying the night air on the portico above the entrance.

To give a definition of the London season that would satisfy a West End lady and inform an inquiring Oriental is not an easy task. The difficulty arises from the fact that the 'season' is not, like other seasons, limited by fixed dates, nor is it the season of any one thing in particular... It is not especially the dancing season, the riding-in-the-Row season, the Parliamentary season, the drum season, the bazaar season, or the garden-party season, but the season of all combined.

The Season was basically a series of events forming the backbone of a society summer allowing members of the aristocracy to mix, mingle, reinforce connections, keep out the riff raff and show off, sometimes a little, often a lot. For the wealthy newcomers to Victorian Society – the industrialists, financiers and manufacturers – the Season's activities helped them to adhere to a set of rules of behaviour which in time would assimilate them with aristocracy of old. Laborious rituals such as 'card-calling', and other forms of etiquette, ensured that those not necessarily born into Society at least were accepted into it on prescribed terms.

In time, the qualifications for belonging to Society were eroded. As entry into politics and the diplomatic service became elective and civil service appointments subject to competitive examination, both originally preserves

A detailed aerial view of social London in the last Season before the Great War. Concentrating on the exclusive areas of Mayfair and Belgravia, landmark London mansions such as Londonderry House, Devonshire House and Grosvenor House are clearly annotated.

8

of the upper classes, the fundamental power base on which Society rested was weakened. Instead the Season took on a glamorous, almost theatrical mantle, with the wealthy and well-born welcoming artists, writers, sporting figures and actors into its ranks to form a cosmopolitan milieu in the years following the First World War. By the 1920s, the pages of society magazines such as *The Tatler* and *The Bystander* show theatrical types or Hollywood stars rubbing shoulders at nightclubs and balls with titled peers and members of the royal family. In the late 1930s the American ambassador Joseph Kennedy brought some transatlantic allure to the Season with his unstuffy, charming family including Kathleen 'Kick' Kennedy, who married William Cavendish, heir to the Devonshire dukedom. At a ball in 1932, the Prince of Wales danced with the aviator Amelia Earhart.

Many events that made up the old London season are still celebrated today, but a number of once-integral activities of the Season have come and gone. The Ranelagh Club, Society's playground and polo venue in Barnes, south-west London, closed its gates in 1939 and was finally demolished after a fire in 1954. Riders may still be occasionally seen today in Hyde Park's Rotten Row, but back in the nineteenth century smartly turned out horsemen and women would nod and bow to acquaintances from their steeds in front of gawping crowds. The weekly church parade, where members of society would promenade around the Stanhope Gate at Hyde Park, might be likened to a red-carpet film premiere today. Glittering parties were thrown by aristocratic hostesses in some of the great mansions of London but most of the houses were either pulled down decades ago and built over, or else are no longer private residences. These places and pastimes are now part of the history of the Season. Most significantly the Royal Courts, or Court presentations, once the pinnacle of the London Season and the most exclusive invite in town, were finally dispensed with by Buckingham Palace in 1958.

The right of entry to the sovereign was a very ancient privilege which had gradually become more restricted over the centuries. Queen Elizabeth I allowed the public access to the long Galleries of Greenwich Palace when she progressed

Mrs Joseph Kennedy, wife of the American Ambassador with her daughters, Kathleen and Rosemary in their court gowns. They were presented to King George VI and Queen Elizabeth at Buckingham Palace at the first Court of 1938.

to church and King Charles II ate his dinner in public. In 1673, Dryden refers to a 'Levee held in a Drawing Room' (the term 'levee' deriving from when the King would arise and dress in front of his advisors) and Queen Anne refers to ladies being presented at Drawing Rooms in her letters. At first presentations did not necessarily focus on young girls, but instead on both men and women, usually after marriage or some form of social or professional advancement. The first record of a number of young girls at Court is during the reign of George III (1760–1820) at Queen Charlotte's birthday ball, held every year at St James's Palace.

By the reign of Queen Victoria (1837–1901), young and newly married women from noble or diplomatic families were expected to be 'presented' to the monarch before making their debut in Society. The ritual came to be seen as the official passport into society, a Certificate of Presentation, first issued in 1854, proof of a well-born young lady's credentials. Following their curtsey in front of the queen at the age of 17 or 18, these 'debutantes', as they came to be known, would, quite literally, graduate from the schoolroom to the ballroom in a matter of weeks. Margaret Haig Mackworth, 2nd Viscountess Rhondda (1883–1958), described in her autobiography, *This Was My World* how, 'I had left school at the end of the April term. In London in May I Came Out.'

This first taste of adulthood was an exhausting round of afternoon teas, receptions, cocktail parties and balls in some of London's most luxurious venues, shoe-horned in and around the main events of the season. Not only

A Drawing Room at St James's Palace around 1750, during the reign of King George III, a period when the formal ritual of court presentation began to take shape.

was this ritual, known as 'coming out', intended to introduce girls into a sophisticated grown-up world (albeit a tightly controlled and chaperoned one), it also covertly signalled her availability on the marriage market. Lord Byron was famously to call the Regency Season, 'The Marriage Mart' and so it remained for the next century and a half.

Even as late as the 1950s girls from a certain background were not expected to be academic or career-driven. Marriage and family were, unsurprisingly, the end goal for many a debutante. The Season was in fact, an enjoyable way for the upper classes to continue to forge dynastic unions.

SEARCY
FOR DEBUTANTE
DANCE SUPPERS

EVERY-
THING
ARRANGED
including
SUITABLE
HOUSE
for
DANCES
WEDDINGS
ETC.

19 SLOANE
STREET,
S.W.1
Tel.: Sloane 3131

Searcy's, still trading today, were the leading caterers to Society during the twentieth century.

But marriage was by no means the sole point of the Season for a debutante. It was, more than anything, a rite of passage and for many it was a memorable and magical period between childhood and adulthood when pleasure and fun were a passport to acceptance. Not everyone enjoyed it, nor saw the point of it, but like many traditions it was done because it simply always had been. As Lady Pamela Smith, a debutante of 1931, put it in an interview in *The Queen* the following year:

> I certainly think a girl ought to be presented, not for any snobbish reason, but because it is one of the few old-time traditions that are left that seem worthwhile. In a sense it is a kind of hall-mark, and, after all, if you are going to be presented you might just as well have all the fun at least of one season. If a girl has the opportunity she is silly to miss it.

Lady Pamela Smith, daughter of F. E. Smith and after her marriage, Baroness Hartwell, was a debutante in 1931. One of the most popular society girls of the period, she was interviewed by *The Queen* magazine in 1932, and gave her views on the advantages of 'doing the Season'.

In twenty-first century terms the Season, as it once was, means very little – a series of sporting events perhaps, but otherwise, a nebulous, hazy concept wrapped in tradition, nostalgia and romance. Vestiges of the elitism that was once an integral part of the Season remain of course, but these events no longer constitute a strict calendar of social belonging. At the very worst the Season was based on a snobbish, elitist premise, played to the rules of rigid etiquette, and existed to uphold class divisions. But it was also a glamorous, quintessentially British concept, meticulously recorded by contemporary writers and participants. It is a fascinating record of how the British upper classes operated and an irresistible opportunity to glimpse a lifestyle of luxury, privilege and quaintly archaic tradition.

The **TATLER**

LADY PAMELA SMITH

THE LONDON SEASON

DOING THE SEASON required the stamina of youth. 'I'm so d_____d tired,' confessed a distinguished but exhausted dowager to *The Tatler*'s correspondent at the end of May 1937, only a third of the way through the busy Coronation Year Season. Though hardly the sort of fatigue experienced by her working-class contemporaries in fields, mines or factories, the Season was nevertheless a gruelling marathon. William Makepeace Thackeray, writing to a friend from Switzerland one July during the mid-nineteenth century remarked, 'Three weeks of London were more than enough for me, and I feel as if I had had enough of it and of pleasure.'

Scores of high-profile events were sandwiched between the Private View at Burlington House in the first week of May and the Season's finale marked by the races at Goodwood at the end of July. The Season of 1913 got off to a good start when, according to *The Tatler*, 'the usual medley of society and Bohemia were present at the private view on Friday last, busy seeing each other and sparing occasional glances for the crowded pictures whose colours were killing each other all over the walls.' For Lady Mary Clive, formerly Mary Pakenham, a debutante in the mid-1920s, it paid to take note of what was hanging on the walls. In her lively memoirs, *Brought Up and Brought Out*, she admitted that for the sheltered debutante with no life experience, the Royal Academy Show was practically the only subject anybody could conjure up at the tedious luncheon parties she was invited to. It would no doubt have preoccupied conversation during the 1930 Season as portraits of four recent debutantes – Miss Rosemary Hope-Vere, Lady Mary Lygon, the Honourable Phyllis Astor and Miss Nancy Beaton – were among the pictures exhibited.

The private view was closely followed by the opening of the season at the Royal Opera House, and when Glyndebourne Opera Festival in Sussex was launched in the summer of 1934 it was quickly adopted as another fixture of the Season, albeit one away from the capital. Glamorous evenings at the theatre may have been a year-round pleasure, but during the Season in particular it was a rather more egalitarian opportunity to mingle with the smart set. In the 1890 edition of *London of To-Day*, a handbook to the capital and

Opposite:
An alfresco
tea outside
on a terrace
at Ranelagh,
as recorded by
the artist Charles
Edward Turner in
1923. A popular
destination
for society,
Ranelagh pleasure
gardens provided
sporting facilities,
refreshments and
entertainment for
adults and children.

An invitation to the State Performance of the Royal Italian Opera in 1897, Queen Victoria's Diamond Jubilee year.

Private View at Burlington House by Gennaro d'Amato in *The Illustrated London News*, 1902. The Royal Academy Private View in the first week of May traditionally heralded the start of the summer Season.

the Season published annually, its chapter on the theatres estimated that on any given night between seventy and eighty thousand people would visit the theatre. It also observed that 'theatre-parties are becoming a fashion of modern London society ... a row of stalls is booked for host and guests; and all drive off to the theatre, after the house-festivities are concluded.' Twenty-three years later, its eighteenth edition commented that, 'Boxes on the grand tier at the Opera House may be bought by any one who will tender a sufficient cheque early enough in advance. To be recognised in a prominent position at Covent Garden Theatre at least once a week in May and June is an object of ambition for many...' adding that, 'Among the functions of the Season may be included the obligation to appear some few times at the theatre in the fullest style of dress you can command.' In other words, the theatre was the ideal backdrop against which to flaunt one's wealth and status.

Proportionally, arts and culture played a small role in the entertainments of the Season in comparison to sporting and social events. Flower shows were popular and during the late nineteenth century a number were held at the Crystal Palace in Sydenham. The Chelsea Flower show, originally the Great Spring Fair based in Kensington, evolved into the Royal Horticultural Show and moved to Temple Gardens by Embankment station. Becoming unpleasantly crowded in the Edwardian period, it found a new home at the Royal Hospital, Chelsea in 1912. At various times, other fashionable sources of amusements

An impression by Cecil Beaton of Edwardian society arriving at the theatre for a first night performance. Beaton himself was at the very heart of the 1920s social scene.

during the Season included listening to the military bands in Hyde Park or St James's Park on Sunday evenings, recitals and concerts, fetes and charity bazaars, a May morning in Kew Gardens or at Hampton Court and meetings of the Four-in-Hand and Coaching Clubs in Hyde Park, a spectacle that attracted thousands each year.

Hyde Park in particular was a magnet for Society during the Season; *Harper's New Monthly Magazine* in 1886 commenting that, 'by the state of the Park an experienced person would at once know the period of the year.' It described 'The Park' as a piece of ground about three hundred yards long and fifty wide, between Hyde Park Corner and Albert Gate, containing a carriage drive, three walking paths and the celebrated riding path called Rotten Row, once known as Route de Roi. It was here at prescribed times that riders would meet, usually between 1 p.m. and 2 p.m. and then later, in the evening when, 'people wear their smartest clothes and ride their smartest hacks'. Such was the densely packed throng that most riders ended up walking, which made the whole process of salutation and conversation easier anyway. For debutantes, or, 'young ladies not regularly in society,' it was an opportunity to meet potential suitors and, 'consequently, a good deal of matrimony is hatched among walkers and sitters.' The quality of Hyde Park's patrons was clear. In May 1913 *The Tatler* spotted Lady Airlie in Rotten Row, Lord Stanley, the eldest son of Lady Derby, watching the horse brigade, and Princess Victoria riding in the Row with her niece Princess Mary.

There was polo at Hurlingham, Roehampton or Ranelagh. Ranelagh in particular, which had the novel distinction of holding a polo match lit by electric light in 1880, offered far more to its visitors, including tea on the

Opposite: The Chelsea Flower Show, still held at the Royal Hospital, Chelsea today, attracted far more than horticultural enthusiasts each May. For Society and royalty, it was an essential date in the Season's calendar.

Hyde Park was transformed into a sea of hats, parasols and fine horseflesh at appointed times of each day when smart society flocked there to see and be seen during the Season. This scene from 1886 replicated itself through the years and by the twentieth century, press photographers would linger in the park waiting to snap famous figures.

The meeting of the Four-in-Hand club in Hyde Park was a highlight of the Season and always drew a crowd of spectators to see the picturesque coaches from the 1840s period assembling in the park for a drive down to Ranelagh.

lawns, amusements for children, gymkhanas and golf. The club was once such an integral part of the Season that magazines regularly ran fashion features suggesting 'Outfits for Ranelagh'.

In any given year, those who frequented Ranelagh were likely to mingle with the same acquaintances at the Eton–Harrow and Oxford–Cambridge cricket matches, the all England Tennis Championships at Wimbledon and the picturesque Henley Royal Regatta. Families with sons at Eton would enjoy the Fourth of June, instituted to commemorate a visit of George III to the school. After speeches, given in Greek and Latin, there would be a luncheon ('excellent', remarked a correspondent of *The Lady* in 1930, 'consisting of cold salmon, galantine, quails in aspic, strawberry ice and hock cup') and the day would always be rounded off by the Procession of Boats on the river and a firework display.

Another highlight of the Season was the Royal Tournament, first staged at the Agricultural Hall, Islington in 1880 and announced in *The Times* as 'a military tournament and Assault-at-Arms'. It was held in aid of the Royal Cambridge Asylum for Soldiers' Widows and brought together volunteers from across the Army in a series of competitions from swordsmanship to tug 'o' war. In 1903, *London of To-Day* declared it 'one of the most interesting of all London's annual shows... It would be a mistake to miss it when in Town.' The show moved to Olympia after the First World War,

Refreshment time at the Eton v. Harrow cricket match by humorous artist Harry Furniss and published in *The Illustrated London News*, 1881. The social side of such traditions often superseded the sport itself.

Equestrian artist, Gilbert Holiday capturing the dynamism of the Royal Tournament at Earl's Court in 1927, with the M Battery of the Royal Horse Artillery performing the Musical Drive in front of the royal family.

where it continued to enjoy popularity. Usually attended by the royal family, the young Princess Elizabeth visited the Tournament in the 1930s and delighted in the riding displays.

Equestrianism of one sort or another was usually a guaranteed draw for royalty, particularly horseracing, a sport that found an enthusiastic supporter in Edward VII. Of the Season's major racing fixtures, the Derby was the festival

of the people. Ascot, conversely, was the festival of the aristocracy and Society's prime opportunity to shine. To gain access to the hallowed Royal Enclosure, a lady would apply to the Lord Chamberlain's office in the same way she would

for May 1932

PETER
RUSSELL

THE MISSES WILSON

For Cup day : Fern-pattern
printed chiffon, with knotted green sash and
halter collar of the two materials. Fox fur, dyed pale pink.

"Engaging" aptly describes
Peter Russell's printed chiffon, with gauged
sleeves and front panel. Baku hat with ribbons to match.

Chiffon dress from Isobel, its
perfect cut and good features accented
by the misleadingly simple black pedal straw hat.

Flower wreaths are a growing
fashion. Ulick's beige chiffon has a wreath
of gay field flowers, repeated on the coarse straw hat.

ISOBEL

ULICK

be required to do so for presentation at Court. 'A pass to the Royal enclosure is eagerly sought after and not readily obtained; still, the enterprise might be attempted by ladies of influence,' advised *London of To-Day* in 1903, adding that it 'is filled with elegantly dressed ladies, whose chief object would seem to be to rival each other in the richness and splendour of their costumes.'

Opposite:
The elegant, graceful bias-cut dresses of the 1930s were ideally suited to Ascot dressing. Here, designs by the Misses Wilson, Peter Russell, Isobel & Ulick are suggested for exactly that by *Harper's Bazaar* magazine in May 1932.

The Charm of the Woman in Black
AS REVEALED AT ASCOT

The Countess of Portarlington and Mr. Lowther

Lady Newborough

Lady Sybil Grant

Lady Knaresborough and her Daughter, the Hon. Helen Meysey-Thompson, and Mr. Miller Mundy

Lady Evelyn Guinness

Earl of Derby with Lady Wolverton

Much has been said of the Black Ascot. The obvious fact, however, that the peculiar beauty of the Englishwoman, particularly the blonde, is never seen to better advantage than in mourning has not been generally admitted. Certainly, rarely or never have the well-known beauties of London Society, some of whom are photographed above, been better appreciated than by their admirers of 1910. Foreign visitors are said to have been particularly impressed on this occasion, and there is already talk of *une mode noire* in Paris.

The fashion crowd of Ascot faltered temporarily in 1910 following the death of racing's most famous patron, Edward VII, but rallied with a dramatic showing of black gowns. *The Bystander* magazine that year seemed quite captivated by the sight, running a full page of photographs.

Studying form was a fairly low priority for ladies at Ascot. During the Season, Ascot dresses were given as much priority as debutante dance frocks and Court gowns in women's magazines. Only the best would do for Ascot and over the years names such as Molyneux, Digby Morton, Isobel, Rahvis, Victor Stiebel, Ella James and Dior were called on for show-stopping attire. Beside Court functions (and perhaps the Fourth of June celebrations at Eton), Ascot emphasised class divisions more than anywhere. 'Being in the Royal Enclosure at Ascot is being on the inside looking out,' explained *Vogue* in 1935, 'every one wears his badge conspicuously pinned to his coat lapel or wrap.

Impressive-looking attendants in green plush liveries stand at the various entrances to the Royal Enclosure to watch with hawk-like eyes and prevent anyone without a badge from passing the iron railings.' This safe haven of exclusivity had the added cache of the annual attendance of royalty and its own small display of pageantry, the traditional carriage drive down the course, is still carried out today.

The royal presence at functions through the Season was what set it apart from those in other countries. *The Tatler* in 1913 admitted that 'Royalty still "makes a difference" even in these democratic days, and charity shows, social functions, the Opera, scintillate with a distinctly brighter brilliance when to their other attractions the chance of the presence of the King or Queen is added.' Forty-five years later the same magazine proudly declared, 'nowhere else offers a combination of attractions so varied as those of the London Season and nowhere else can provide that essential ingredient – the British monarchy. For it is the Queen – and the spectacle and ceremony that go with her presence – who lifts the London Season above all competition.'

It was perhaps, with a sense of relief that the Season drew to a close at the end of July. Livelier supporters of the Season would go on to Cowes on the Isle of Wight for the regatta, but after that there was one direction in which Society headed, and that was north, to the moors of Berwick and beyond for the start of the shooting season. Whereas it was essential to be seen *in* London during May, June and July, suddenly it was just as important *not* to be seen there in August. Christopher Petherick, joint managing director of Searcy's, caterers to Society, claimed that people would get in a month's supply of food, close the windows and shutters and fake their own disappearance from the capital.

August brought discernible changes to the capital. Cabmen and waiters underwent a transformation from haughty to humble once their bountiful sources of income had departed and it was, for the ordinary mortal, 'delightful … to dress as he likes, walk where he likes (even within the sacred boundaries of the "Row"), eat and drink what, and at the time, and how he likes … without loss of caste, or danger of being outlawed.' For the author of *London of To-Day*, the exodus of the capital's 'quality' guests meant a welcome return to normality.

Society of course still followed its own timetable. Country-house weekends, particularly in the Edwardian era, lasted from Saturday to Monday and the shooting season overlapped with the hunting season, which in itself generated a series of balls and parties ensuring a continuous supply of photographs to the society columns. There was, in certain eras, a 'mini Season' from September to November – a sort of warm-up for the real thing – but by the 1920s and 30s the smartest began to seek out warmer climes during the winter months.

Opposite: Pageantry at the races – King George V and Queen Mary riding in a carriage past the grandstand at Ascot in 1927. The ultimate race meeting for the 'Sport of Kings', Royal Ascot's close association with the monarchy is celebrated each year by the traditional carriage drive down the course.

HOW TO BE A DEBUTANTE

URING THE HEYDAY of the debutante there was no such thing as a teenager. Loelia Ponsonby, later Duchess of Westminster, spoke for many debutantes when she wrote in her autobiography, 'Till one came out, one was a child, the same as one had been ever since one stopped being a baby, speaking when spoken to, dressed in any old clothes (it went without saying that well-dressed children had common mothers) and of course with no male friends.'

The transformation then, from ugly duckling to graceful swan, needed to be swift, and spectacular. Unsurprisingly there was plentiful advice on offer. Magazines such as *The Girl's Realm*, *The Lady* and, especially, *The Queen* ran regular articles about what to expect from the Season, how to behave at Court and what sort of investment should be made in a debutante's wardrobe. *The Queen* in 1932 featured an article, 'Right Clothes to Wear for Every Occasion: Requirements of a Debutante's Trousseau, and Some Hints on the Art of Sensible Buying' by one Louise Andree Coury. Ms Coury recommended drawing on the experience of a woman who had already brought a daughter out recently to ensure the whole thing was done properly. And mindful of many of *The Queen's* more wealthy readers, she added, 'Of course if the mother prefers she can go to one of the well-known Court dressmaking houses'. But for those with more 'average circumstances', she recommended a modest outlay of attire and accessories which totalled £223, the equivalent of around £12,000 today, with furs, or clothing for the sports-loving debutante, increasing the cost further. For parents with several daughters to bring out, the associated costs must have been truly alarming. It was a state of affairs summed up merrily by Adrian Porter in the 1938 book of humorous verses, *The Perfect Debutante*.

It is of course the proper thing
To make your curtsey to the King
Arrayed by Molyneux or Worth
Whether of fat or slender girth.
(A debutante who little owns
Can safely go to Peter Jones).

Opposite:
A debutante of 1902 arrives at a photographer's studio following her presentation at court. Many of the leading studios remained open late into the night in order to cope with demand after court presentations moved to evenings during the reign of Edward VII.

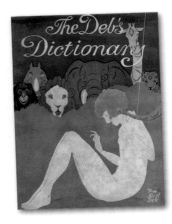

The Deb's Dictionary, by Oliver Herford, was a humorous anthology of the terms used in the debutante's world in the 1930s. The naked deb, waking up in the Garden of Eden is suggestive of the transformation from naïve ingénue to sophisticated society lady within the space of one Season.

The Duchess of Westminster, appearing on the front cover of The Tatler, in 1930, the year she married the fantastically wealthy 2nd Duke of Westminster. However, as a debutante in the 1920s, she made many of her own clothes and re-covered her worn-out dancing shoes.

It is unlikely that every debutante amassed quite such a sophisticated array of garments. Loelia Ponsonby made a number of her own clothes admitting that, as it was the 1920s, 'nothing had to fit', and even re-covered a pair of shoes herself (which wore out quickly due to all the dancing), dipping the heels in red ink and laboriously stitching the black satin. Ladies of the 1890s were advised in *London of Today* that Miss Kate Reily of Dover Street was the doyenne of London dressmakers, but did recognise that those with thrift 'will not have recourse to the Leading Dressmakers'.

Fiona McCarthy, who recalled her experiences as one of the last of the debutantes to make their curtsey to the Queen in 1958 in *The Last Curtsey*, had a dress from Worth for her presentation, but the rest of her coming-out wardrobe included more conventional labels such as Susan Small and Frank Usher. She remembered one girl whose dressmaker copied his wealthy clients' Balenciaga designs, and was able to spend her first Season looking distinctly fashion-forward. Lady Diana Manners made her own train when she was presented at court from 'three yards of cream net sprinkled generously with pink rose-petals' and wore a 'curious dress … my own copy of a Lucille model' at a Court ball in 1911, which, due to its insecure stitching, came a little undone during a Royal Quadrille and had to be hastily fixed with her Coronation medal.

Conversely, the ravishing Henrietta Tiarks (later Duchess of Bedford), who came out in 1957, was an only child of rich parents. She wore a pink dress, decorated with fabric blossoms, by couturier Pierre Balmain for her coming-out dance. Another only child from a wealthy background, Miss Margaret Whigham (later Mrs Charles Sweeny and then Duchess of Argyll), led the cohort of more sophisticated debutantes in the 1930s with her effortlessly chic wardrobe: 'I was lucky enough to have

THE DUCHESS OF WESTMINSTER

an extremely generous father and a mother with impeccable taste... I was allowed to order a dozen beautiful evening dresses and many day outfits (awful word!) for the Derby, Ascot and the many lunch parties to which I would be invited. Most of these clothes were made by two young men just down from Cambridge – Norman Hartnell and Victor Stiebel – both of whom were later kind enough to give me credit for helping to launch them on their way to fame.'

She wore a Hartnell creation for her coming-out dance in 1930, of turquoise-embroidered tulle. Tulle was one of the fabrics recommended by Hartnell in an interview with *The Queen* magazine in 1932 where he advised the debutante on her choice of court gown. Tulle, he declared, in white or pastel colours, was, 'suggestive of youth and unsophistication' while for those past their teens, chiffons and soft satins

cost of a débutante's trousseau as outlined above :

	£	s.	d.
Lingerie, including 4 sets underwear, 1 dressing gown, 2 bed-jackets, 1 corset or belt made to measure, 9 pairs stockings	35	0	0
Shoes and gloves, including 6 pairs of shoes and 10 pairs of gloves	20	0	0
2 morning suits or ensembles, with berets or hats to go with them	15	0	0
2 afternoon outfits, ditto	25	0	0
Afternoon frocks for Ascot, etc., with hats to match	25	0	0
3 silk washing frocks	9	0	0
3 Evening dresses	30	0	0
Plain wool coat to go over tennis frocks	4	0	0
Afternoon wrap	10	0	0
Evening cloak	10	0	0
Various accessories	10	0	0
Presentation gown, train and veil	30	0	0
Total	£223	0	0

The list of attire and accessories recommended for a debutante's trousseau, published in *The Queen* in 1932.

were more suitable. He went on to list feather fans as preferable to bouquets ('which can wilt in the heat'), no jewellery except a string of good pearls ('I consider it the height of bad taste for a young debutante, or any unmarried young woman who is being presented at Court, to wear ostentatious jewellery'), and attached great importance to 'the right foundation garments.' Hartnell clearly enjoyed the process of designing a debutante gown, remarking how he was 'often amazed at a girl's quick transformation from the schoolgirlish stage to the young woman who is able to wear her clothes with the unconcern of an accomplished mannequin.'

Anyone uncertain about how to dress for the Courts could enquire at the Lord Chamberlain's office for particulars. Reville Ltd were court dressmakers to Queen Mary, and in the decade leading up to the First World War were one of the premier couture houses in London. During King George V's reign, it was therefore Reville which was asked to submit a design for a gown which adhered to court regulations and which could be displayed at St James's Palace for ladies to consult. Trains, which had once trailed behind Victorian debutantes like a peacock's tail, were shortened to no more than eighteen inches from the heel after the First World War, partly as a post-war expression

of economy, partly to speed up the curtseying debs, who could move faster when unimpeded by acres of silk satin. The more faddish elements of fashion were forbidden, or at least frowned upon – hobble skirts of the Edwardian era for example, or, as Lady Eleanor Smith advised in *Vogue* in 1927, 'it is unwise

Opposite far left:
A court dress
of ivory satin by
Reville of Hanover
Square, published
in *Harper's Bazaar*,
1930. A favourite
of Queen Mary,
Reville was
frequently
chosen to design
Palace-approved
sample court
dresses at the
beginning of the
Season, which
would then be
displayed as
guidance to ladies
attending court.

Designs for
court gowns by
five of the leading
fashion houses
of the twentieth
century, illustrated
by Reynaldo Luza
in *Harper's Bazaar*,
1933. From left
are exquisite
dresses by Reville,
Victor Stiebel,
Isobel, Norman
Hartnell and Enos.
Hartnell found
great fulfilment
in designing
dresses for a
girl's presentation
gown, admitting,
'I feel when I am
designing it, that
I may have some
part in forming
that girl's destiny.'

to choose an exceedingly short dress', but within these boundaries, ladies could modestly follow the latest fashions, or add signature touches. When David Lloyd George's daughter Olwen was presented in 1913, her gown bore an embroidered Welsh harp in soft shades of gold, pink and green.

Olwen Lloyd George, daughter of chancellor of the Exchequer and future prime minister, David Lloyd George, photographed in her court presentation gown in 1913, embroidered patriotically with a Welsh harp.

Opposite: Front cover of *The Queen* magazine's Débutante Number from 1932, depicting a debutante waiting in her car in the Mall with Buckingham Palace in the distance, where she will be presented. Society magazines placed great importance on the Season and the central ritual of court presentations, and frequently ran these 'special' numbers each year.

As well as the all-important presentation gown, there was hair and make up to consider too. The advent of bobbed and shingled hair in the 1920s brought challenges for the society hairdresser who began to incorporate 'transformations' – pieces of false hair – into the owner's real hair at the back of the head, in order for there to be something into which to secure the three ostrich feathers (representing the Prince of Wales) that ladies at Court were obliged to wear until the late 1930s. Emile of Conduit Street were old hands at this sort of hair-styling, warning debutantes in their advertisements that, 'The most perfect hairdressing is vital for your presentation. Our experts, trained by many years' experience, are at your service for your Court coiffure and the correct attachment of your veil and feathers.' Jean Stehr – Court Hairdressers, assured potential clients that, 'particular attention to the requirements of debutantes is being given.'

Cosmetics were considered 'fast', though some debutantes of the inter-war years were allowed a little powder only to stop shiny noses (a Victorian debutante would not even have thought about it). Some got away with lipstick ('lipsalve') in subtle rosebud shades, but anything more was thoroughly discouraged. Face creams and manicures seem to have been accepted by the 1920s and 1930s, so a girl could look well groomed rather than wanton. Some society girls even dabbled in endorsement with both Rose Bingham, later Countess of Warwick, and Princess Marina of Greece, the future Duchess of Kent, advertising Pond's Cold Cream. A spritz of scent was allowed of course – L'Aimant by Coty was a popular new fragrance in the late 1920s, or perhaps L'Acaciosa de Caron (Parfum de la Jeunesse – perfume of youth); by the 1950s, *The Sketch* was recommending fresh fragrances such as Vent Vert by Balmain and Worth's Je Reviens.

The clothes, the hair, the face – all was of the utmost importance if a deb was going to make a good impression, both in the ballroom and in the papers.

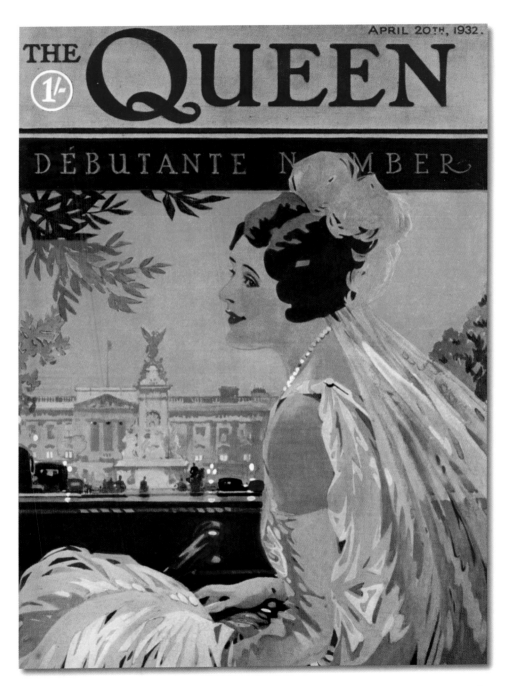

Looks were a debutante's currency, a fact all too obvious from reading the opinions of society columnists. They had few qualms about assessing each new Season's girls by their appearance — who was the 'prettiest', whether this Season's girls were more attractive than the last, and who was a contender for 'Deb of the Year', the qualifications for which seem unclear. Of 1932's debutantes *The Bystander* sniped, 'On the whole they were not as pretty as last year. There was rather a lot of puppy-fat.' *The Sketch* in 1958 devoted large amounts of space to photographs of debutantes such as Penelope Riches who was described as possessing a 'model-girl figure, and great grace and poise,' Lois Denny who was, 'as pretty as a piece of Dresden china' and Penelope Butler-Henderson who was 'dark and strikingly beautiful'.

The prettiest debs would be given starring roles at Queen Charlotte's Ball and at the Berkeley Dress Show. Debs were cruelly categorised according to their looks; the most attractive one selected to be the 'bride' and model a wedding gown at the show's finale, while plainer girls were consigned to sell programmes and clap politely.

If looking the part was essential for your first Season, then acting the part took equal prominence. Most debutantes received a lacklustre education but many were sent to finishing schools on the Continent (usually Paris or Switzerland) before doing the Season. Here they would combine some cultural experiences such as visiting museums and galleries, with learning the language, but also flower arranging, entertaining, public speaking and deportment. Even as late as the 1950s a girl pursuing a serious, academic education did not advertise it widely. It simply wasn't done to be clever. *The Sketch* magazine, in its 1958 Debutante Number recorded that, 'At Mrs O'Rorke's lunch, I met mothers of "blue stockings",' specifically Teresa Hayter and Fiona McCarthy, who had been accepted to read modern languages and English respectively at Lady Margaret Hall, Oxford. Though congratulatory, the tone was politely surprised. By singling these girls out as 'blue stockings', *The Sketch* was making it clear they were a different breed. Others refused to conform in alternative ways. Unity Mitford, presented in 1932, frequently took her pet rat, Ratular, to dances, or her pet grass-snake, Enid, as a novel, living necklace.

Imagine Unity's scorn at the thought of lessons in the art of curtseying, which was seen as imperative. For those presented in the years between the First World War and the late 1950s there was only one place to go – Vacani's School of Dancing at 159 Brompton Road, Knightsbridge. It was founded by Marguerite Vacani and her sister, who perfected the art of the graceful curtsey for thousands of would-be debutantes.

Unity Mitford, notoriously to befriend Hitler a few years after her presentation, showed her non-conformist character during her first Season by taking her pet rat or snake to balls and parties. She purloined some writing paper from Buckingham Palace when she was presented and took delight in using it.

The school was given added cache when it tutored the young princesses Elizabeth and Margaret Rose in dancing lessons. Before Madame Vacani, Victorian debutantes would be schooled in the art by Mrs Cowper Coles, in the dancing room of her flat at 31A King's Road, Sloane Square. Here they would learn to manipulate train, bouquet and fan, and memorise a diagram of the Drawing Room at Buckingham Palace, with dots denoting where the Queen and other royals would be positioned. So rigorous were these Court rehearsals that her pupils considered them as 'muscularly fatiguing as any outdoor game.'

This newly acquired grace and poise should be recorded for posterity, and so for every debutante a trip to a photographer's studio formed an essential part of her

Betty Vacani (1908–2003), principal of Vacani's School of Dancing (and neice of its founder), the foremost school for dance and deportment in the country. Miss Vacani taught countless debutantes to curtsey, as well as the royal children, including Prince Charles, Prince of Wales, how to dance.

A lady is tutored in the art of gracefully dropping to a curtsey during her presentation at Court at the school of Miss Cowper Coles in 1899. A piece of tartan fabric is a makeshift train and a bunch of chrysanthemum act as a substitute for the debutante's bouquet.

coming-out season. Though several portrait sessions might occur during the Season, the photograph of a debutante in her presentation finery was the one most likely to appear in smart magazines. Long-established society photographers such as Bassano, Vandyk and Speaight extended their opening hours to cope with demand immediately after presentations. In the *Debutante and Court Illustrated*, 1926, Speaight Ltd advised customers that, 'on Court nights the studios remain open until 1 a.m. … clients wishing to meet friends after the court can arrange to do so at the galleries.' Back in 1890, ladies were advised in *London of To-Day* that it took about quarter of an hour

Front cover of *The Sketch* magazine from 1950 summing up the social whirlwind of the Season, and the necessity for debutantes to become 'quick-change' artists.

" THE MERRY, MERRY MONTH …"
… when debs. become quick-change artists.

to photograph a lady in Court dress, also that 'Stout people are the most difficult. They have to be fined down, and their waist rounded off in the negative.' The fashionable portrait photographer Madame Yevonde took hundreds of debutante portraits, including those of Hon. Unity and Jessica Mitford. In 1932, she carried out a photo essay for *The Queen* magazine entitled, 'A Day in the Life of a Debutante', a slightly mocking depiction of a typical twenty-four hours for a 1930s deb, from waking late and having a manicure, to lunching with mother and, in a case of life imitating art, visiting the photographer.

Typically, the fruits of these photographic sessions would appear in one of the society magazines, announcing to the world (or at least to those who read *The Queen* or *The Tatler*) that a girl had made her debut. Grandmothers who had made their curtsey in the Victorian era regarded the practice of appearing in the papers as rather vulgar. Mary Pakenham, a debutante in the 1920s, confirmed this: 'Debutantes weren't ever written up. None of us had a press cuttings book and it was considered dubious, if not positively vulgar, to allow a studio portrait of oneself in an illustrated weekly.'

But appear they did, and from the 1920s onwards increasing numbers of debs would have their photograph published in the society pages. Looking back at the faces in these pictures, from the vapid grace of pre-war debutantes to the sensible head-girl types from the 1950s, it is worth remembering that each of them will have endured — or enjoyed — similar preparations for their coming out. Even into the late 1970s, when court presentations were very much a thing of the past, the famous Lucie Clayton College in Kensington continued to prepare girls for marriage, society and the Season. Regardless of the era, coming out required a complex recipe of shopping, fittings, beautifying, deportment, etiquette and, to a certain extent, publicity to turn the gauche schoolgirl into (in Maud Rawson's words) a 'maiden of quality'. Once the transformation was complete, it was time to officially 'come out' in Society.

A debutante visits the photographer — one of a spread of tongue-in-cheek vignettes — showing a day in the life of a debutante by society photographer Madame Yevonde, 1932.

THE COURTS

THE DISTINCTIVE RED TARMAC of the Mall, in central London, linking Buckingham Palace at its western end to Admiralty Arch in the east, was created as a ceremonial route, a flag-bedecked conduit for royal processions and a gathering point for crowds at events of national importance. For the debutante it had special significance too. It was here that she would spend several hours, waiting nervously, perched in her finery and feathers on the back seat of a smart car, as it crept forward at a painfully slow pace towards its final destination – the Palace.

The long line of cars (or carriages, depending on the period) snaking, nose to tail, down the Mall, carrying their precious debutante cargo, was a familiar sight when the Season was at its height. Several Courts were held each Season, in May and June. The number was dictated by how many presentations were requested, but generally there would be three or four, with one usually devoted to ladies connected to the diplomatic service.

It was a spectacle that attracted attention not only from newsreel crews and press photographers, but also from crowds of onlookers curious to see first-hand these butterflies about to emerge from their chrysalises. For any shy debutantes, the waiting must have been something of an ordeal. Not only were they on the verge of being presented to royalty – a nerve-wracking thought for all but the most confident – but spectators could get a little too close for comfort. *The Bystander* magazine in 1927 reported,

With each Court, too, the crowds of sightseers increase, and now cars-a-bancs come up specially from the outer suburbs and from even further away, bringing hundreds more to gaze upon the befeathered matrons and maids sitting in the long line of motors.

It is not pleasant to be stared at for three hours – or longer if you are in the first flight of cars – as if you were a new strange animal at the zoo, by an endless procession of people. But it doesn't end with staring. Some of them mount the footboards of the cars in order to get a better view.

Opposite:
The sight of debutantes waiting in their cars in the Mall was such an integral part of the Season, it was employed by Dunlop Tyres for one of their advertisements in 1928. Note the policeman on horseback – there to ensure the crowds of spectators did not press up to the cars too closely. Travelling to central London to scrutinise the waiting debs in their cars was a popular pastime, with some travelling in from the suburbs in charabancs especially for the occasion.

More venturesome souls, apparently thinking this waiting is for their especial benefit, actually open the doors.'

Back in 1899, Maud Rawson, writing 'On Being Presented' in *The Girl's Realm*, alluded to a similar problem when she described a debutante 'becoming conscious of an audience – of all sorts and conditions of men – eagerly scanning the carriages'.

To pass the time while queuing, many ladies waiting to be presented brought along something to do. In 1932 *The Queen* magazine carried photographs of debutantes amusing themselves in various ways. Some of the more bold debs quaffed champagne, happily opened the doors and posed for cameras. *The Lady* magazine suggested (somewhat disapprovingly) that, '...in all probability they are enjoying themselves wildly.' Mrs Rawson imagined her late Victorian debutante whiling away the hours by nibbling on 'a fancy basket of miniature sandwiches' placed on the back seat by 'a thoughtful maid.'

In her tightly gloved hand, a debutante would be holding her all-important presentation card, guaranteeing her entry into the Palace. She and her sponsor would have applied to the Lord Chamberlain's office at Stable Yard, St James's Palace, for these precious pieces of card. Sponsors would be ladies who had already been presented and who, after a seemly period of three years, were in a position to introduce a young woman herself. They were usually mothers,

Many debutantes brought diversions to pass the time spent waiting in the Mall. Knitting, backgammon, listening to a wireless or even recording the scenes with a cine-camera were all captured by The Queen magazine in 1932.

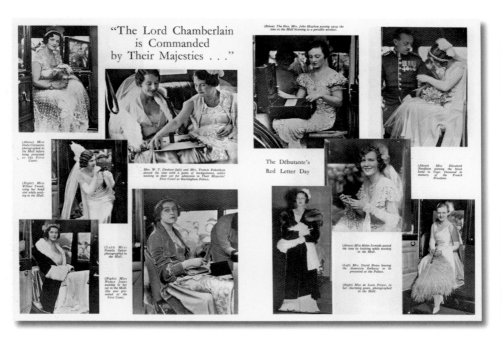

"The Lord Chamberlain is Commanded by Their Majesties . . ."

The Débutante's Red Letter Day

but might also be aunts, elder sisters, distant relations, friends or, often, impoverished peeresses who made a living from presenting the daughters of those families rich enough to pay their way into society but without the vital social connections. Access to Court presentations was rigidly scrutinised before admittance, as Loelia Ponsonby, later Duchess of Westminster, recalled. Loelia was the daughter of Fritz Ponsonby, Head of the Royal Household, and consequently came into the royal orbit frequently. She was presented to George V and Queen Mary in 1925 but remembered how her mother presented another girl at the same time whose own mother had been divorced and so could not appear at Buckingham Palace. The names of all those presented at court (as well as at levees – confined exclusively to men) would be listed in *The Times* the following day.

During the reign of Queen Victoria presentations were made at afternoon drawing rooms, held either at Buckingham Palace or St James's Palace at 3 p.m., with no refreshments on offer for the wilting debs and the only source of 'comfort' a chamber pot placed behind a screen. Often considered the invention of the queen, in fact the afternoon drawing rooms were a legacy of her uncle, George IV, who no doubt felt he had better ways to spend his time in the evening. The elderly queen would often find the ceremony just as gruelling as those waiting, and typically endured the endless curtseys for a couple of hours before retiring and passing the baton to the Princess of Wales, or one of her

A cross-sectional drawing of Buckingham Palace showing carriages arriving at the West Portico entrance, and the route up the grand staircase, through to the ballroom where presentations were most frequently held during the 1920s.

PALACE GARDENS

BALL ROOM
where courts have been held in previous years

DRAWING

ROOMS

PICTURE GALLERY

THRONE ROOM

STAIRCASE

ENTRANCE CORRIDOR

WEST PORTICO ENTRANCE

A debutante presented to Queen Victoria during an afternoon drawing room in 1887, the queen's Golden Jubilee year. Court regulations stipulated deep necklines and short sleeves, unless a lady was known to be too delicate to come to court except in demi-toilette in which case she could wear a high bodice and elbow sleeves.

daughters, who would act as proxy in her absence. Unsurprisingly, competition to be presented early on – and therefore to Victoria herself – was fierce and things could get ugly in the anterooms, with a certain amount of unladylike jostling to secure a prime position. In 1930, long after Victoria's reign, *The Lady* wrote knowingly, 'The early debutante catches the worm, the worm in this case consisting of a chair in the throne room, the occupant of which can amuse herself by watching all the other ladies as they make their curtsies of varying ease and distinction. This is obviously vastly more amusing than waiting about outside the throne room after presentation – as those who come later are obliged to do for lack of space.' At the first Court held by the new Princess of Wales (the future Queen Alexandra) in May 1863 at St James's Palace, an extraordinary 537 ladies were presented. Some endured a six-hour wait in their carriages before, 'they attained, jaded, worn out, and dispirited, the privilege of being admitted to a pen, to wait under genteel coercion, for an hour or two longer.' 'The hustling and the pressure was so great,' said Lady St Helier, 'that many gowns were almost destroyed before the wearers reached the Presence Chamber where the Princess of Wales stood.' Much jewellery was apparently lost in the crush.

Lady Diana Manners (later Cooper) was presented at Court in 1911 and happily jumped the queues as her mother, the Duchess of Rutland, had been given the 'entrée' by Queen Victoria when the former was nursing her first baby. The privilege remained in force for life meaning Lady Diana did not 'spend three hours queuing … to the main door of the Palace,' but could 'stalk in through a smaller but nobler entrance.'

Once assembled in the ante-room precedence was given to the daughters of peers, who went first and were rewarded by a kiss on the cheek from the queen, an action that required them to manoeuvre themselves and their four-foot train into a position close enough for the diminutive monarch to reach down. 'You had to make a deep curtsey to get down low enough,' explained Lady Clodagh Anson, who was presented in 1898.

The rest were expected to kiss the queen's hand and, depending on the number of members of the royal family present, the debutante might find herself curtseying several times (though Mrs Rawson points out that four curtseys would certainly suffice). All the while she needed to ensure she did not turn her back on the queen as she edged politely but gingerly away from the royal presence until safely out of sight. Attendants were on hand to help with the cumbersome trains, working expertly to unfold it as a lady moved into the presence of royalty and then placing it back over her

A series of sketches from *The Illustrated London News*, 1893, observing the stages of a debutante's first drawing room, from the wait in the Mall and the crush of the anterooms to negotiating the long train with the help of attendants and kissing Queen Victoria's hand upon presentation.

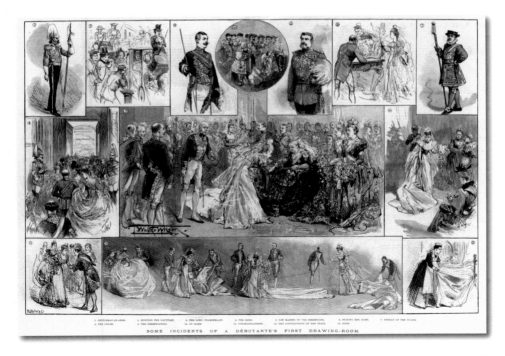

SOME INCIDENTS OF A DÉBUTANTE'S FIRST DRAWING-ROOM.

arm as she left. Some debutantes managed to carry off this ritual with aplomb. Margaret Whigham even managed to exchange a flirtatious glance with Prince Aly Khan, who stood on the dais behind Queen Mary. 'For a split second our eyes met before I had to turn and walk away from the throne. I wondered who he could possibly be.' Fortunately, she met him the following evening at a ball at Brook House given by Lord and Lady Mountbatten where they 'danced every dance together', the beginning of a brief love affair that was ended abruptly when her parents refused to give their consent to his proposal of marriage.

Presentation at Court, the high point of the Season for a high-born young woman, and for many the defining moment of their relatively brief lives, lasted just a few seconds. Loelia, Duchess of Westminster, described the ceremony as,

> ...over in a flash. One reached the head of the queue, handed one's invitation to a splendid official, he shouted aloud one's name and tossed the card into a rather common-looking little wastepaper-basket, one advanced along the red carpet, stopped and made two curtsies to the King and Queen who were sitting on a low dais surrounded by numerous relations, and then walked on.

Mrs Rawson remarked on how the 1899 debutante was left with one impression: 'the extraordinary brevity of the supreme moment – this great appearance before her Majesty, which has coloured the debutante's dreams for weeks. Are all supreme moments to be as short as this?'

For some the 'supreme moment' was even shorter. The brief reign of Edward VIII ushered in a more informal approach, expressed by the decision to hold presentations in the garden of Buckingham Palace. In principle, the notion of Society's first ever open-air Court seemed rather charming, with the debutantes in their long, bias-cut dresses and hats making their curtsey on the lawn in front of the king, who sat underneath an exotic red and gold Indian shamiana. Unfortunately the British weather lived up to its reputation. As the heavens opened, the debs of 1936 rushed towards the shelter of the refreshment tents, more drowned rats than social butterflies. A week later they received a letter from the palace explaining that, due to the unforeseen inclement weather, those who had not managed to make their curtsey should nevertheless consider themselves presented. It must have been a disappointing anti-climax after months of anticipation.

Debutantes of the Edwardian era enjoyed a far more dignified ceremony in opulent surroundings, described nostalgically by *The Queen* in 1922 as the 'imposing, beautiful and enjoyable

Front cover of *The Perfect Debutante*, a book of humorous verse and sketches from 1937 showing a blushing debutante in disarray after an ill-timed trip. A stumble in front of the monarch must have been every debutante's nightmare, though reports of such incidents usually observed that the king and queen maintained absolute composure, and calmly ignored any hiccups in the ceremony.

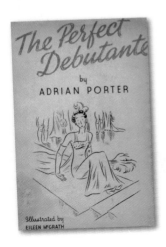

The Perfect Debutante
by
ADRIAN PORTER

Illustrated by
EILEEN McGRATH

functions over which Queen Alexandra presided during those twelve years of social brilliance.' Afternoon drawing rooms were re-invented as evening Courts, where the silks and satins of the debutantes, and the jewels of their chaperones, glittered under the palace's new electric lights, and nervous appetites were sated by champagne and a generous buffet. Though always a subject of interest in the illustrated papers, the Edwardian debutante began to take centre stage, the subject of countless illustrations by magazine artists such as Balliol Salmon and Lucien Davis.

The Courts of King George V carried on in the same way, until the advent of war in August 1914 brought a sudden, though temporary, halt to proceedings. For four years there were no presentations, and even when the war was over it took some time for the Season to warm up again. In early May 1919 *The Queen* wrote, with barely concealed excitement, 'While the nations were at war, the King deemed it unsuitable to hold any State function of a social nature, and to this view his Majesty adheres; but so soon as the Final Treaty of Peace is signed, it is anticipated that at least two evening courts will be held at Buckingham Palace…'

The King and Queen held garden party courts that year in order to deal with the number of presentations, 'rendered inevitable by the four years of war, during which no Courts were held' sighed *The Queen*, though it reported that, once the initial deluge was dealt with, 'the King and Queen will resort

Overleaf:
The Supreme Moment by Balliol Salmon in *The Bystander*, 1928, showing debutantes making their curtsey to George V and Queen Mary.

Below: The brief reign of Edward VIII introduced a more modern form of outdoor court presentations, but the inclement British weather ruined the 'supreme moment' for many debutantes who were obliged to run for cover when the heavens opened.

to the plan of earlier days, and will hold courts in the throne room of Buckingham Palace. This will no doubt be a popular move, for every bride and debutante naturally prefers to have an individual presentation – unless, indeed, she is subject to exceptionally acute attacks of shyness.'

A year later the evening courts were back, but it was not until 1922, with the restoration of full court dress (the traditional feathers and a train 18 inches from the heels of the wearer, but with the new, fashionable shorter skirts allowed to be five inches off the ground), that it was felt that there was a return to normality. *The Queen* summed it up by admitting, 'Even the fact there is an authoritative dress once more is a delight; for there is no doubt that the psychology of dress is a factor of considerable importance, and the fact of making one's curtsy in a specially-prescribed frock adds to the pride and satisfaction of the occasion.' Clearly *The Queen*, a society bible and reverential chronicler of each season, felt far more comfortable when there were rules by which to abide.

After the 1936 debacle, it was with some relief that the new king, George VI, and the charming Queen Elizabeth reinstated the evening courts, where Helen Vlasto remembered partaking of a 'lovely buffet supper laid on by Lyons' afterwards. There were some modernising concessions. *The Tatler*

A reproduction of *Their Majesties' Court, Buckingham Palace* by Sir John Lavery, painted in 1931 and exhibited at the Royal Academy in 1932. Lavery took individual portrait sketches of many society ladies and debutantes in preparation for the work, which gives an excellent impression of the scale of court presentations in the Palace's ballroom. The painting is now lost.

A charming illustration by Rex Whistler from around 1930, caricaturing some of the main protagonists of a court presentation day – the shy but excited debutante, the matronly dowager chaperone and the eager crowds gathered to witness the spectacle.

remarked at 'the striking innovation of the new reign when all the ladies in the Royal circle appeared for the first time without veils and feathers.' But, as the clouds of war gathered over Europe, it was clear that Royal Courts would be short-lived, and for many the presentations of 1939 were seen as Society's last hoorah. Post-war presentations were once again relegated to afternoons to cope with the mundane logistics of managing numbers – debs and their mothers wore smart day dresses and demure hats instead of shimmering silk evening dresses. Princess Maureen Ghyka, daughter of the Romanian diplomat, Matila Ghyka, who was presented in 1938, perhaps best summed up the lost magic of this defining ritual. She recounted her experiences of the Season in a series entitled, 'Out of the Chrysalis' in *The Queen* the following year.

> When the long-awaited moment at last came and I was actually making my curtsy, I really don't know why, but it was the only thing in my life that did not disappoint me, simply because it was my earliest dream come true.

Miss Ghyka's moment would have surprised Charles Eyre Pascoe who, writing in *London of To-Day* in 1890, all but consigned court presentations to the dustbin of history when he wrote:

> Colourless dowagers and shivering damsels are now called upon to don evening or ballroom attire on cold spring mornings and present a ridiculous spectacle to ribald spectators in the Mall and St James's Park. Perhaps old Court customs and modern Court rules had better be left to antiquaries and gentlemen ushers. In the light of day they seem a little ridiculous; and doubtless, in a few years to come, will be merely interesting as the gossip of history.

But court rules and customs had staying power; it would be another seven decades before Pascoe's prediction would finally come true.

DANCING AND ROMANCING

FOR HER Birthday Ball, held each year at St James's Palace, Queen Charlotte, consort of George III, liked to be surrounded by family, friends and her maids of honour. The highlight of the celebration would be the presentation of a large cake, lit up with candles, carried in ceremoniously to the strains of Handel's *Judas Maccabeus*. It was this historic celebration that provided the blueprint for the resurrected Queen Charlotte's Ball, launched by the redoubtable Lady Howard de Walden in 1925 in aid of the maternity hospital bearing the queen's name. Unsurprisingly for an event with roots in the eighteenth century, the resulting ritual, rigorously rehearsed beforehand, was somewhat quaint and faintly absurd. Dressed entirely in virginal white, the scores of debutantes would march in solemn procession behind a huge cake (contributed by Jackson's of Piccadilly) decorated with electric candles, the number of which symbolised the years since Queen Charlotte's birth. In one seamless ripple of snowy white, the assembled young ladies would simultaneously dip into a low curtsey in front of the cake before it was cut by the Dame d'Honneur, who was either a member of the royal family (Princess Beatrice in 1930, her niece Princess Helena Victoria in 1958) or a lady of society (one year Lady Diana Cooper, another the Dowager Duchess of Northumberland, on another occasion Lady Churchill). Some years the prettiest debs would be chosen to pull the cake in on wheels, while their less glamorous peers were given the job of distributing the cake. Aside from the prestige of attending, each debutante would receive a present; 1939's gift was a bottle of scent from the glamorous house of Schiaparelli.

If Queen Charlotte's Ball was an oddity, or 'absolutely idiocy' as one deb put it, it was, by the 1930s, an essential date in the Season's calendar for a debutante, and it did, after all, raise considerable sums for its chosen charity. Unlike most other facets of the Season it continued through the Second World War – though the cake was made from dried eggs – and took on a greater significance after the demise of court presentations in 1958.

There was also the Royal Caledonian Ball, established in the 1840s by the Duke and Duchess of Atholl to entertain their circle while in London.

Opposite:
The Royal Caledonian Ball, a taste of the Highlands in the heart of Mayfair.

Beaming
debutantes in their
traditional dresses
of virginal white
wheel a huge cake
onto the ballroom
dance floor at the
Grosvenor House
Hotel during
Queen Charlotte's
Ball, 1959. The ball
was a highlight
of the debutante's
Season, particularly
after court
presentations
ended in 1958.

Held in the capacious Grosvenor House Hotel ballroom from 1930, the Caledonian was unashamedly Scottish, with men dressed in Highland attire and the first reel piped in by the Duke's personal, private army, the Atholl Highlanders. Besides these perennial fixtures, there were scores of other balls and dances filling up each Season, many of them supporting a myriad of worthwhile causes, adding an increasingly altruistic aspect to the Season.

Most debutantes would also have their own coming-out dance at which they were, at least for one night, the belle of the ball. By the 1950s, these were often shared with a sister, cousin or friend for reasons of economy, and they were carefully timetabled so as not to clash with any other parties. Jennifer, aka Mrs Betty Kenward, society columnist for *The Tatler*, and later, *Harper's & Queen*, was an integral element in these arrangements. Anxious mothers would visit the *Tatler* offices to consult her diary in the weeks leading up to the Season. In 1928 'Mariegold' in *The Sketch* reported on an anxiety of

a different sort; 'over the mumps epidemic which has broken out among the young folk, but I haven't heard actually of any "buds" going down with the fell malady imported by young brothers from Eton.' Two years later it sympathised with poor Lady Kitty Fitzmaurice, daughter of Lady Lansdowne, who had succumbed to measles meaning the fate of her dance, scheduled for 6 May, was uncertain.

The Duchess of Argyll, then Miss Margaret Whigham – quickly proclaimed 'Deb of the Year' by the national press when she came out in 1930 – took the audacious step of holding her coming-out party on 1 May, just as the Season was starting. It was a risky strategy: 'for once all the other debutantes had been to my dance, it was possible that their mothers would not bother to invite me to theirs.' Her fears were unfounded and, 'for the rest of 1930 I received plenty of invitations.'

Margaret's parents held her party at 6 Audley Square, a house they had rented for the Season. Renting large houses suitable for entertaining was common practice among families who lived out of town. For one-off Seasons this was a practical solution, but after renting a house in Gloucester Square for his eldest daughter Nancy's debut, Baron Redesdale, father of the six Mitford sisters, deduced it would make financial sense to buy a house (in Rutland Gate, overlooking Hyde Park) to bring out his remaining five daughters, not perhaps quite the extravagance in 1926 that it might be in the twenty-first century, and modest in comparison to the magnificent Londonderry House on Park Lane, bought by the 3rd Marquess of Londonderry in 1819 as a home for his family during the Season.

As far as accommodation for parties was concerned, the bigger the better was the view of most. Cocktail parties, an inter-war years invention, evening receptions or 'drums' as they were known in the Victorian period, could be tolerable in the more average-sized abode, and by the 1950s it was common for parties to be held in, albeit elegant and spacious flats in exclusive postcodes. The majority of merely 'smart' balls were held in London houses, characterised by an oblong front room adjoining a square back room, giving most balls a certain similarity which, 'usually, from its narrow dimensions, prevents them from attaining the excellence of a ball in a "big house",' remarked *Harper's New Monthly Magazine* in 1886 which went on to describe the desperate and uncomfortable crush in the dining-room while supper was served, leaving the 'more timid to withdraw from all attempts to obtain food,' and for the remainder to 'squeeze themselves round small tables, or stand,

TO HAVE A DANCE GIVEN FOR HER, MISS MARGARET WHIGHAM.

Margaret Whigham makes her debut in *The Sketch* with a front cover portrait by society artist, Olive Snell. Deb of the Year in 1930, she remained a fixation for the press throughout the 1930s. She became Mrs Charles Sweeny after her marriage to an American golfer, name-checked by Cole Porter in 'You're the Top'.

disconsolate, eying the expanse of heads for a vacant space.' The supper-time rush seems to be a repetitive theme. In the 1930s *The Lady* magazine was still describing 'the immense, continual and petulant supper queue.' What a contrast then to be invited to a ball thrown by 'great people', in a gilded and marbled house; from the elegant and calm ascendance up a grand, wide staircase woven with flowers, to a terrace, balcony or garden lit by Chinese lanterns where revellers could cool off.

In her memoirs, Margaret Whigham recalled receiving invites to balls or receptions at Brook House (home of the Mountbattens), Londonderry House, Holland House in Kensington, Sunderland House on Curzon Street and Warwick House. They were glittering affairs and for many defined the Season. 'The complete abstinence from entertaining which is a feature of most English ducal houses has a marked effect on London social life,' complained *The Tatler* in 1913, adding snobbishly, 'it is the chief cause of the rapid rise of the NOUVEAUX RICHE in our midst.' But whether it was the nouveaux riche or the bona fide aristocracy holding balls, after the Second World War, the number of grand mansions in London was fast decreasing. 'Aristocracy no longer keep up any state in London, where family houses hardly exist now,' wrote Nancy Mitford in her essay, *Noblesse Oblige*, while the diarist Chips Channon wistfully reminisced about the last great ball at Holland House in 1939, held for debutante Rosalind Cubitt, and attended by George VI and Queen Elizabeth. Increasingly, by the 1950s, hotels such as Claridge's, Grosvenor House and The Dorchester – some of them ironically built upon the foundations of the demolished mansions – became the more typical venues for the Season's balls and parties. Buffets, champagne, flowers, entertainment in the form of a band (Ambrose and his band in the 1930s, Tommy Kinsman in the 50s) – all added to the eye-watering expense. *The Sketch* in 1957 gave estimates of at least £1,000 for a dance at a West End hotel, while '£4,000 was by no means an unusual figure.' (around £75,000 today).

Despite the magnificence and expense, many debutantes found balls an ordeal, not least for the unnerving prospect of having contact with the opposite sex. Although the Season was ostensibly built around the need for aristocratic young men and women to meet each other, the reality was rarely dignified or romantic. Mary Pakenham gave a withering description of the menfolk on offer in the 1920s, who she considered as clumsy as they were ugly: 'It was of course considered very vulgar for a man to dance well (like talking French at school with a French accent) and, if by any chance one did meet a man who did it beautifully, one was absolutely safe in writing him off as a bounder.' Deborah Mitford described her partners at dances as 'chinless horrors' who spent most of the dance treading on her feet.

To make matters worse, any romantic transactions were often carried out under the watchful gaze of a disapproving chaperone or hopeful mother.

Opposite: Guests ascending a stately and flower-bedecked staircase inside a London mansion to attend a reception during the London Season. The space afforded by the largest houses lent 'dignity and repose to the gathering' and meant that invitations from society's leading hostesses were eagerly sought.

A garden party
at Holland House,
pictured in *The
Illustrated London
News* in 1872.
Holland House,
originally known
as Cope Castle,
was a glittering
social centre in the
nineteenth century
and the scene
of one of the last
grand balls of the
pre-war period.
The majority of
the house was
destroyed during
the Blitz.

For many girls, their chaperone would be their mother, some of whom were
only in their late thirties themselves, and young enough to enjoy their
daughter's first Season. Margaret Haig (Viscountess Rhondda), a particularly
reluctant debutante, remembered arguing with her mother about what time
it was appropriate to go home during a dance (Before supper implored
Margaret – AFTER supper was the firm response). The actress Joyce
Grenfell, then Joyce Phipps and a niece of Lady Astor, made her debut
in 1928 and was, 'never allowed out alone. If my parents were not going
to the dance, I was escorted by the family maid.' Loelia Ponsonby, whose
mother 'had kept her figure and her beauty and was a "dancing mother"' gave
a mischievous description of the majority of chaperones in her memoirs:
'Very fat or very thin, covered with unclean jewellery and showing a good
deal of décolletage, they sat on the stiff little chairs staring through their
lorgnettes and hoping that some old buffer would take them down to supper.

A caricature
of the London
Season: the stout,
bejewelled
dowager, staring
disapprovingly
through her
lorgnette at her
debutante charges.

They were generally referred to as the Dowagers and were
supposed to be of appalling respectability...'

Mollie Acland, a debutante in 1939, said of her own mother,
'I could always tell what sort of chap I was dancing with by her
expression – smiles for rich young lordlings, down to positive
frowns for penniless subalterns!' They were also on hand to veto
nocturnal excursions to nightclubs, and Lady Elizabeth Scott (later
the Duchess of Northumberland) remembered creeping back to
Londonderry House in the early hours of the morning only to be
confronted with her friend's mother, the Duchess of Marlborough,

at the top of the grand staircase. Honesty being the best policy, she threw herself at the duchess's mercy and admitted she had been to the Four Hundred Club, pleading meekly, 'Terribly sorry. Don't tell Mummy'.

As at any event of the Season, the presence of royalty was guaranteed to cause a ripple of excitement. 'Hope runs high in many a hostess's breast just now,' chattered *The Tatler* breathlessly in May 1913, 'in consequence of the rumoured presence of the Heir Apparent at some of the dances of the seas. For a royalty that dances is a lion to catch indeed…' When his brother, Prince George, attended Queen Charlotte's Ball in 1932, he shook hands with every deb present, 'some of whom appeared quite overwhelmed.'

Lady Diana Manners, though celebrated as one of the great beauties of her day, found her experience of dances as painful as many others when she came out in 1911:

> The young girls were raw and shy, innocent of powder and on the whole, deplorably dressed. Shoes were of pink or white satin and were smudged after the first dance by clumsy boys' boots.

> We poor creatures suffered great humiliation, for between dances we joined a sort of slave or marriage market at the door, and those unfortunates with few friends or those who had been betrayed by a partner, or were victims of muddling the sequences of dances, became cruelly conspicuous wall-flowers.

In her lively memoirs, Lady Mary Clive (née Pakenham), spoke witheringly of her experiences of the ballroom during her first season, wondering 'How was it possible for mortal men to be so UGLY?'

Seventeen years after her own debut, Lady Diana held a coming-out dance for her husband's niece, Deirdre Hart-Davis, at 34 Grosvenor Street, lent by Mrs Rupert Beckett whose 'café au lait ball-room made a very good setting for the many pretty girls who came…' wrote Mariegold in *The Sketch*. The Prince of Wales and his brother Prince George 'looked in through the course of the evening' but one wonders if the debutantes of 1928 still felt the same awkwardness as their pre-war sisters.

The self-assured Margaret Whigham guaranteed she was never a wallflower by implementing the Whigham system; filling her dance card up early on with the names of anyone who asked her, but happily displacing them in favour of a more debonair partner, feigning mix-ups or being unable to find the original partner when the time to dance arrived.

The problem of mustering up enough eligible young men to make up the numbers at debutante gatherings preoccupied debs' mothers through the decades. Inevitably there was a sliding scale of preferences, from the top rung of titled aristocracy, moving down to younger brothers in noble families, and then to the so-called 'deb's delights'; well-behaved, well brought-up young men who could be relied upon to make up the numbers. Notices alerting male students to forthcoming debutante balls would also be pinned up in the medical and law faculties of universities, a fail-safe guarantee, if only because it was an opportunity for free food and drink. Occasionally, the society magazines would temporarily shake off their obsession with debutantes and feature their male counterparts. In 1958, the twenty-six-year-old Duke of Atholl (in obligatory kilt), Prince Alexander Romanoff and future Conservative MP Peter Tapsell were all featured in *The Sketch* under the title 'Debutantes' Escorts'. Names of suitable male escorts would be featured on 'The List', shared by debutantes' mothers; struck off unceremoniously if they became engaged and with annotations next to certain names who were deemed 'NSIT' (not safe in taxis) or 'MTF' (Must Touch Flesh). From this personal selection of male escorts to the chaperone system, it is clear that the organisation of balls and parties fell almost entirely to mothers. Most fathers were relegated to the essential but ultimately peripheral role of financial benefactor during their daughters' coming-out.

A selection of eligible bachelors from 1932 featured in *The Queen* magazine, offering a counterpoint to the perennial photographic parade of debs. In the bottom left-hand corner is Randolph Churchill, son of Winston Churchill.

The expense, the preparations, the hand-wringing and the exhaustion; was it all worth it? How many debutantes actually enjoyed the Season, and how many of them actually bagged the prize of a husband? The London Season was also the wedding season (though May weddings, considered unlucky, were less common) and it was significant that magazines often followed their 'Debutante' number with a 'Brides' number. Two years after coming out, Margaret Whigham accepted a marriage proposal from the Earl of Warwick but broke it off after the invitations had been sent out. When she finally married American golfer Charles Sweeny in February 1933 at Brompton Oratory, the crowds assembled to catch a glimpse of the couple stopped traffic in Knightsbridge. Deirdre Hart-Davis married Ronald Balfour at Westminster Cathedral in April 1930. Most girls were married within two or three years of their first Season. Some were quicker. Diana Mitford was engaged to

These Eligible Bachelors and . . . .

Top row : Sir Basil Bartlett, Bart. ; Viscount Moore. Second row : Lord William Taylour ; Sir Michael Duff-Assheton-Smith, Bart. ; the Marquess of Donegall ; the Duke of Northumberland. Third row : Mr. Randolph Churchill ; Lord Forrester ; Viscount Knebworth.

Photographs by Lenare, Hay Wrightson, Paul Tanqueray, and Vanodé

The wedding of
eighteen-year-old
Diana Mitford and
Bryan Guinness
in January 1929.
Diana sulked until
her unwilling
parents finally
agreed to the
marriage. Just
over a year
later, she was
photographed
for *The Sketch*
with her baby
son Jonathan.
The couple were
divorced in 1932.

the fantastically wealthy Bryan Guinness within a few months of her first
Season. Three years after their marriage, the couple were divorced. For most
young girls marriage seemed to
be the only clear path to take,
and offered an escape from the
close surveillance of the family
home, but the comparatively
high rate of divorce was telling.
Immaturity, inexperience and
a sense of duty led many young
debutantes up the aisle in
haste, and left them to repent
at leisure. But others were
luckier. Sir Martyn Beckett
spotted Priscilla Brett dancing
a whirling waltz at a debutante
ball in 1939 and told his
companion that was the girl
he was going to marry. Their
union lasted until Priscilla's
death in January 2000.

The Hon.
Priscilla Brett,
third daughter
of Viscount and
Viscountess Esher,
who as a debutante,
caught the eye
of architect
Sir Martyn Beckett
at a ball during the
1939 Season. The
couple's marriage
lasted from 1941
until Priscilla's
death in 2000.

THE LAST PARADE

O N 20 March 1958, the last presentations were held in the ballroom at Buckingham Palace. As the debutantes arrived, defiantly wearing thin, spring dresses despite the biting weather, two young men drove up the Mall in a vintage 1920s Rolls-Royce, brandishing a placard inscribed, 'Good-bye, dear debs.' Strictly speaking, there were to be two more presentation events that Season, a garden party for Commonwealth debutantes in July as well as a presentation party at Holyrood House in Edinburgh, but for the media, and for the majority of the two thousand debutantes who rushed to be presented that year, 20 March marked the end of an era.

An elderly spectator, interviewed by *The Times*, seemed disappointed at the parade of debs shivering in their chiffons and silks; 'It isn't the sight it used to be,' he sniffed. 'In the old days, they wore tiaras, and jewels and feathers,

Debutantes and their parents queue up outside Buckingham Palace for the last court presentations in 1958 on a freezing March day. Onlookers remarked disappointedly on the prosaic appearance of the debs in comparison to those of past decades.

it was really something to see.' His companion added, 'it's just a load of snobbery. It's a good thing it's come to an end.'

The word from the man on the street had not gone unnoticed. The end of presentations was part of a modernising drive at the Palace and an attempt to ally the monarchy with the burgeoning meritocracy that was beginning to shape the Fifties. Many debs accorded the blame for this decision towards Prince Philip, who made no secret of his zealous wish to give the more anachronistic elements of his wife's job a good spring clean. The excuses made were polite and diplomatic; the queen's schedule prevented her from meeting all the debutantes who applied and that her many engagements had to be devoted to people from more varied sections of society. Princess Margaret's view of the debutante scene was considerably more barbed. 'We had to put a stop to it,' she is said to have quipped, 'Every tart in London was getting in.'

To many Society ladies who had made their curtseys back in the glamorous days of the 1920s and 30s and were now bringing out their own daughters, the death knell of court presentations came as no surprise. Margaret, Duchess of Argyll, who had been the irrepressible deb of the year

Scene from Vincente Minelli's film version of *The Reluctant Debutante*. The popularity of the play and film, which gently satirised the debutante scene, chimed with changing attitudes, and was instrumental in eroding the respect held for the tradition.

A spread from *The Tatler*, reporting on the lavish dance held at Claridge's for debutante Frances Sweeny in 1955.

in 1930, accompanied her daughter to the Palace in 1955 noticing that, 'Gone were the beautiful evening dresses and jewels of the women and the dress uniforms of the men. Debutantes were now presented at afternoon parties, and it was therefore in a short dress that Frances made her curtsey to the Queen, the Duke of Edinburgh, the Duke and Duchess of Gloucester and the Princess Royal.' The sheer mundanity of these courts were an acute contrast to her own experiences as a debutante and she noted, 'it was brought home to me how the splendour of the 1930s had vanished for ever.'

In the same year, the William Douglas-Home play, *The Reluctant Debutante* opened at the Cambridge Theatre in May. Starring Anna Massey, who had herself been presented at Court that Season, the play was a gentle satire on the clichés of debutante life, from the pushy mothers to the put-upon fathers. It was not, as Fiona McCarthy puts it, 'that the Season's silliness, or even its venality had never been admitted, but it rated as a private, relatively inbred joke. William Douglas-Home's play, later turned into a movie by Vincente Minelli with Kay Kendall and Rex Harrison, made the family secret embarrassingly public. What could a deb do now except plead reluctance?' The prestige and pride of being a deb was rapidly beginning to fade and after 1958, once the glossy mantle given to the Season by its royal ceremonial high point was lost, increasing numbers of girls were forgoing the Season entirely.

There were plenty of other reasons the Season began to lose its appeal. The times were changing at a rapid rate and the Season found it hard to keep up.

An education became something to strive for rather than conceal, and a number of would-be debutantes found that the Season clashed inconveniently with their exam timetable. For others, the Swinging Sixties scene made the archaic traditions and mannered rituals outmoded and laughable. It was the decade of free love, drugs, long hair, and most importantly, anti-establishment satire. Jennifer, *Tatler*'s social diarist, must have been bemused to find herself impersonated by Fenella Fielding on *That Was The Week That Was*.

Pop music began to displace the house bands of hotels, and with formal ballroom dancing abandoned, and the music too loud for polite conversation, dances no longer had the cross-generational appeal of former times. As Valerian Wellesley, Duke of Wellington, observed in a 2001 television interview, 'I don't see the point of dancing six feet away from each other. The whole point was to get hold of a girl.' Tommy Kinsman, who had been the favourite bandleader for coming-out balls in the 1950s admitted, 'The kids wanted to do the opposite to what their parents did. They called everything old-fashioned.'

But for those who had made a living from the Season, it was time to display a very British stiff upper lip and carry on regardless. Jennifer in *The Tatler* regarded the lack of presentation courts as 'a minor respite … the Season will go on just the same and people will wonder whatever made them think it was going to be so different.' She was poached by *Queen* magazine in 1959, but she was becoming as antique as the system she chronicled. The magazine devoted more space to mocking the debutantes they had once feted, publishing articles by young writers such as Charlotte Bingham, who poured scorn on her own experiences of the Season in her 1963 novel, *Coronet Among the Weeds*, and Jennifer found the space allocated in the magazine for her diary beginning to shrink. Nigel Dempster, renowned diarist for the *Daily Mail*, commented acerbically on 'Jennifer's' merits. 'It is horrendous to think she considers her diary a "record of life." If the Martians only read that, they would think we were inhabited by freaks and freeloaders.' Meanwhile, *The Tatler* continued to cover the London Season, but in 1963, instead of a society 'gal', iconic model Jean Shrimpton appeared on their cover, albeit in a ladylike Otto Lucas hat.

The Season did carry on, in a fashion. The Berkeley Dress Show continued, though the girls modelled bell-bottoms alongside evening

Former Deb of the Year Henrietta Tiarks modelling for California Cottons in 1960. She gave up modelling, and a potential acting career, to marry Robin Russell, Marquess of Tavistock, later the 14th Duke of Bedford. The responsibility of running the family home, Woburn Abbey, left no room for a personal career.

61

gowns, and the word 'debutante' had been dropped from the title by 1973. Queen Charlotte's Ball lasted, held at the Grosvenor House Hotel and helped in part by Peter Townend of *Tatler* (now owned by Condé Nast) who would ring up mothers to ask if their daughters were going to do the Season – as if the 1960s had never happened.

In the inevitable circle of life, the ball was revived in 2009 by Jennie Hallam-Peel and Patricia Woodall, 'anointed successors of Peter Townend' according to the *Daily Mail*. The new Queen Charlotte's Ball scours two exclusive London schools for their 'debutantes' and the old tradition of wearing white dresses – and the mass curtsey – remain. There is even a deb of the year, usually somebody who has distinguished themselves with outstanding charity work or contributions to the community. The emphasis is on raising money for charity and the organisers have brought in several 'luxury brand' sponsors to augment the £250 ticket price; Fulham-based wedding dress designer Philippa Lepley provides the voluminous gowns, Maserati transports the girls to the venue, and Japanese pearl specialist Mikimoto is responsible for the jewellery. In Paris, the Bal de Debutantes at the Crillon Hotel was brought once more to life in 1992 and features the daughters of rock stars and Hollywood royalty, dressed in high-couture gowns in which they are photographed for endless technicolour spreads in *Hello!*. These extravaganzas seem rather silly and irrelevant in the twenty-first century, and strangely reminiscent of the elitist discrimination forming the foundations of the original 'Debutante Age'. Perhaps the debutantes of yesteryear find it all terribly vulgar? Though they may approve of *Country Life* magazine, still running their famous 'Girls in Pearls' frontispiece featuring a girl who may not be a debutante, but could very well have been had she been born seventy years earlier.

Even Tatler began to reflect the social changes of the 1960s in its covers. Model Jean Shrimpton posed for their 1963 London Season number, and other covers showed working women fitting in a lunchtime hair appointment, or students at a new university. *The Tatler*'s owners sold the title in 1964 and replaced it with the short-lived but achingly hip London Life.

The majority of ex-debs look back on their coming out and the Season with fondness, but concur that it is has no place in today's society (with a small 's'). By and large, the debutante is a historical curiosity. Of her presentation in 1939, Peggy Cripps admitted in a documentary on the debs of that year: 'I'm glad I did it. Glad I went to Buckingham Palace as it was such fun but it was an archaic idea really.' The debutantes inhabited a gilded, romantic but ultimately outmoded upper-class world. And while their stories stir up a mix of nostalgia, envy and even outrage in this more democratic age, the ghosts of past Seasons still have a fascinating tale to tell. Lady Bowman, another debutante of 1939, summed up her memories of doing the Season and should have the last word; 'It was lovely and it was magical – and all magical things come to an end.'

FURTHER READING

Fiona McCarthy, *Last Curtsey* (Faber & Faber, 2007)
Anne de Courcy, *Debs at War* (Phoenix, new ed. 2012)
Anne de Courcy, *1939: The Last Season* (Phoenix, 2003)
Margaret Pringle, *Dance Little Ladies – Days of the Debutante* (1977)

The return of the debutante? Modern-day debs at the revived Queen Charlotte's Ball, perform in choreographed unison in the magnificent surroundings of the Durbar Hall of the Foreign & Colonial Office in London's Whitehall.

INDEX

Page numbers in italics refer to illustrations